by Sharon M. Luster

Printed in China

ISBN-13: 978-0-15-362405-6

ISBN-10: 0-15-362405-1

8 9 10   0940   15

4500519938

Harcourt
SCHOOL PUBLISHERS

Visit *The Learning Site!*
www.harcourtschool.com

What People Need

A zoo worker tosses food to black bears. Someone in your school waters a plant that is sitting on a window sill. A squirrel runs up a tree to its leafy home. Living things need food, water, and places to live. People need these things, too.

The world we live in has everything we need to survive. There are plants and animals for our food. There is water for us to drink. We can build our homes out of wood from trees. All of the things that we use are called resources. Some resources cannot grow back after we use them. We need to use resources carefully so that there will always be enough of them.

Resources
People, animals, and plants use many of the same resources. Can you find some resources in this picture?

lake

soil

forest

People Cause Changes

As people use resources, Earth changes. People clear forests for building towns. They cut down trees for wood. They turn soil to plant crops. Sometimes their factories release waste that makes rivers and lakes dirty.

So, some of these changes do harm Earth. But people can make changes that help, too. Sometimes one person can help. Sometimes people get together in groups to help. You might have some ideas about how you can help.

er

ocean

beach

Water

Drinking isn't the only way we use water. People need clean water for cooking and washing. Many factories use water when they make things. Firefighters use water to put out a fire. People like to fish or swim in water at beaches, lakes, or rivers.

Every year, the people of Cleveland, Ohio, have a celebration because their river is now clean. Years ago it was dirty. There was a great deal of oil and factory waste in the water. The oil in the water caused fires to burn on the river. Pictures of the fires were in newspapers and magazines. Everyone knew that this was a terrible problem.

Water Use

This chart shows how much water one person uses. How do these amounts compare to the amount of water that you drink? ▶

Amounts of Water Used

Activity	Water Used
Take a bath	50 gallons
Take a 10-minute shower	20 gallons
Brush teeth	1 gallon
Wash hands	1 gallon
Flush toilet	3 gallons
Run dishwasher	20 gallons
Wash dishes by hand	5 gallons
Washing machine	10 gallons

Helping Animals Live

Plastic dumped in the ocean washes up on beaches. It often looks like food to a bird or a turtle. But plastic gets stuck in the animal's throat or stomach. It can cause the animal to starve.

So people made laws to keep waste out of the water. Slowly the river got cleaner. Today, people in Cleveland still work to keep the river clean. Now they can go fishing and boating.

Some groups help keep oceans and beaches clean. Clean Ocean Action is made up of many different groups of people. Clean Ocean Action did its first beach cleanup in 1985, and 75 people came. Now thousands of people help pick up trash from beaches around the country. Clean Ocean Action tries to teach others about oceans. The group also works to get more laws made that will help to protect oceans.

Land

There is only so much land for living things to use. But every year there are more people in the world. They need more resources from the land.

Farmers work to grow enough food. Crops use nutrients in soil to grow. Many farmers use the soil carefully. They may let a field rest and not plant anything, or they may plant another crop that uses different nutrients in the field.

Some farmers raise cattle. These animals eat grass. Farmers move the cattle from place to place to let the grass grow back. The roots of plants hold the soil so that wind and rain cannot carry it away.

Cutting wide steps into a hillside makes flat places for planting. It also keeps rain from washing soil down the hill.

Planting Trees

After forest trees are cut, a machine pulled by a tractor plants small trees. The machine cuts the soil. The worker puts the tree in the ground. The two tires in back push the soil down around the tree.

Forests are another important resource. Many animals make their homes in forests. People use wood for houses and furniture. The paper in this book came from trees. Foresters often plant new trees after cutting down older trees. The new trees can be used by people many years from now.

The leaves of trees help the air. One group of schoolchildren started planting trees in their city. They got others interested in helping. Today, children all around the United States belong to this group. The children have planted one million trees, and they are still working. The first small group even started a recycling center.

You Can Help

Some of these stories may give you ideas about what you can do to help. You do not have to be a grown-up to make a difference. All you need is an idea. Are you interested in oceans or forests? Would you like to help a place near where you live? You may want to talk to friends or classmates about your idea. Your teacher or someone in your family can help you, too.

When you decide what you want to do, try to get other people interested. You can have a lot of fun as you make good changes to help the world.

The Three Rs

Reduce. Buy things without extra wrapping that creates trash.

Reuse. Use things again instead of just throwing them away.

Recycle. Turn in glass, metal, and plastic to a recycling center. ▶

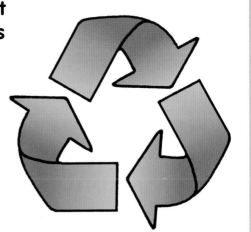